AF615181

Art in the 7th Power

Poems
Corinne Robins

Art
Phoebe Helman

PRATT PRESS
New York, NY.

The poem "Invisible Books" was first published in *Artist & Critic.* The poem "In the Nest" first appeared in *Confrontation* magazine.

Library of Congress Catalog Card Number
86-61473
1 CORINNE ROBINS
Title: ART IN THE 7TH POWER
ISBN: 0-930557-00-X

With special thanks to Elizabeth Marraffino, Larry Joseph and Ingrid Wiegand.

Thanks to the Art Department, Pratt Institute, Brooklyn, N.Y. 11205

Cover and book design: Joan Snitzer

Pratt Press
83 Wooster St.
New York, N.Y. 10012

For Sal

CONTENTS

Art in the 7th Power

1.

Six months into 1970
in undeclared war,
the New York Art Strike—
400 people on the Metropolitan steps
with studio-pale faces—demand free museum entry.

In June, going up lower Broadway,
policemen follow on horseback.
Not everyone loves a parade,
only the marchers,
their faces filling the sky.

Nights near the falling hotel,
three bears look out on transvestite
  walk.
Noons, a catatonic sun
catches the welfare people
In situ against a building.

Afternoons, we improvise graffiti days.
White walls turn dull cream,
hearts on floor, our shrinking minimal hopes
don't help to cross the street.

I watch TV politics, a child's first day at school
swell to a ten-year sentence.
Living through the 70s,
the span of one whole history.

Seven: lucky spatial shape,
up, and slide across.
A box of time tipped,
playtime—no sign or pointer.
Child, a two-way mirror.

2.

Are you in my time?
"7 is the number of the young light,"
the *I Ching* says, and I ask again,
because if you believe in match-stick time,
things will happen.

Sequins, flowers, stones
celebrate, decorate gallery walls,
expressing wo-man in decade's power mouth,
where waistlines, paint, tongues thicken,
where half-way to hunger,
my roof leaks money worries
in ears of little wars.

Child and mother—teens and twenties
sit for her. In her middle-woman time,
watch Princess Justice, Lady Hope
climb to lucky 7 stand
in subways scribbled red.

Monochromatic walls in supermarkets
  remain the same.
Price a food, a pace, this length.
Snow storms strip the park,
the sun's gone and dying marriages go on.

Play *Grateful Dead* in jet and silver,
smoking something.
Remember no-touch dancing, death-collecting—
from the green corpses of Jonestown's Eden
distancing ourselves.

3.

Seven shadows walk building walls,
years in cases,
another and another skin.

Buttons bud in fine white air,
small leaves feed.
Balloon rides through clearing
as bodies emerge doing drugs, children.
Under planes of change,
we water our lives.

I'm looking in the 70s,
learning hostage manners,
my rockstar legs shaking.

7, dicey number made for hope.
Children leave school in pairs.
Ride buses met by herds of mothers
who lead them in parade.

Ten years of love lost in crumbled minutes.
I have retained my heart.
He builds ideas in my head.
Through pools of sex,
we walk toward age.

4.

Trade, barter sex, advise forgiving mothers.
March madam, lady, woman on the run.
Turn in price of grace,
mirror eyes of other,
sister is not daughter
become nation suspect of girls and women,
all the sex our mothers made us.

Day goddess, woman raging,
singly lonely live.
Cry sadness of menstrual grief.
Cry cow days going.

Maid-in-form, goddess-in-hate,
Fly-us Steiman,
she to soar warrior-faced,
carving here vagina plates,
in seventy times our lipstick eaten off.

Move till movement becomes direction:
Public stars on pedestals drive down
  female cause-ways
I take a private course,
become learned in crying;
hair full of feathers,
fly female and alone.

Move till moving becomes direction:
all our lovers leave, our daughters betray.
The decade becomes, grows
in a ten-year dancc,
with 7 the rising number
of my fading generation.

5.

In '76, some wars are won.
Art temples of water, metal, basement
  stone appear.
Money flows and
utopia gets stoned,
missing God among these voices.

In 7th quest,
we trade prayer rugs for painting,
cult for culture.
Photograph purple baby mannequins,
shoals of irridescent fish
falling on walls and chairs.

In 7th quest,
we hunt make-do religion
using mantras and breviaries
as locks for meditation
while born-again rain falls
and Christians go door-to-door
protesting plural Gods.

In decade where no word saved
and friends were lost
despite karate moves that stilled,
ballet steps that firmed,
I believed in a year's holly bush,
an annual cemetery visit where my father loves,
the future where my daughter lives,
in messages on finger-ends
uttering prayers of art.

6.

Count on calendar cycle:
separation of weeks,
sleep cycle in nights.
On 7th day of 7th month,
tied to astrologic wind,
give me a count.
No poetry without belief,
music without number.

Count out babies born,
unnumbered sperm losers.
On bank check, give a sign,
write in a figure,
a year to death,
my magic, missing number.

Up to ten and down again,
uno, dos. . siete.
Series builds position,
Ten years gone forgets us.

Apartment windows equal—
amoebic mass,
molecular statistic dance.
Faster than decade can remember,
ten years gone forgets us.

Three bears, two geese, one lover,
we used up combinations—
back to front, sideways:
closed doors total
no loves added.

&7

He built a fence across California.
She made tunnels for the sun.
A moment when traffic is less than wind,
when breath becomes visible
the visual took sides
became me, us, cat sound in song,
the charting of internal weather hung
on museum walls.

In 7th power, water kept nothing down.
I discover shoulder pains, adults,
children in running shoes cross my heart,
Body tune-up, breath implosion,
language dissolving,
paintings reach from a wall
mapping verbal problems.

As art divides into day, week, year,
in love now with forgotten moments,
look in future toward past meetings.
Card deck of years,

page plays deconstructed like orgasms,
70 through 79 inhabits certain photos,
backward mirrors meant to summon self,
which isn't art,
but sound and sense bîts
in someone's memory pocket.
No one home.

Shut down paintings, make room:
what things revolve are laid out
  differently
for, because, being a seventh time
believed as someone's moment—
a time before certain childhoods
whose accordion days were yours—
are gone
with fucking and being fucked for art.

So, in 7th time,
in 7th day, week, month, sign,
end begins meaning,
power of young light changing—
all we know, unmade world buried
feeds him, her—
is someone's story
become holy food in desert season,
power watering ground.

—End—

Burned Spaces 1984
92″ L × 60″ H collage, paper paint

December 1983

Living in Power City
with leafless trees in lights
and heads of winter colds.
Beginning season
with good faith berries blooming,
he did drop during dinner, a famous man,
in sleeping, dying day.
Fifty-four years old,
December tabloids said.
Twenty-one days till solstice,
winter pause:
one gone among the flakes,
the seething stores, cash cheer,
long hours and short sun.

Here, under white-blue skies and breaths,
the indoor crowding,
escalator changes,
heavy fed and fleshed
in new-bought skins,
blood ribbons and green pines,
we marshal forces
to celebrate
the interim, in-between,
ungrowing moment
of rusting cold.

Mindwinter

Gray rain's endless arriving
soaks through day.
The city is in shrouds
and I'm writing
by way of not sleeping here
where water is a moving light,
a silver-cast on roofs and sidewalks.

Is Paris full of pools?
New York rain at 7:00, at 9:00
the cold at 1:00 sends minds in frozen time,
seeking hot insides of coffee shops
their tropic lights—
till back to cold where breath sings,
bundling, bless us, wind-travelled seeds,
our swaddled bodies
feasting, foraging, aswim in the wind
   among high-building forests.

But now mostly shut in cases, cars,
the air we drink beating at our skins,
our gentle organs, eyes, ears
courage in retreat,
we wait.

An ice shell holds the sun,
our February sentence.
The day at five: radiator steam
rises, sighing, sings
on top of wind: a migrained head,
a sinus head band, winter wear
accompanying our journeying.
So many stops from bed,
so many steps.
Buy yellow tulip suns,
play Haydn's morning music
and, holding winter skins around,
wait to wake till spring.

Which new mind

Which mind begins—
who sits, stops
bent on brain spoil,
5 years, 2 days of hospital
   time between,
she stands mind-blown.
While still I'm here, though
the out-of-sight bird does not return,
may not return, she says,
broken steps still rising
and ruins sun-washed,
walking on healing grass.
Thought ticks and talks.
Terrible time of mind:
invisible things laid waste,
building stories not saved.
Before her now
the house comes down
and in asylum park
the homeless wander—
while guards and insects watch,
tearing at healing grass.

Crazy Isn't Far

Crazy is near, not alien.
A mad dog isn't transformed,
legs and tail are intact.
Eyes, maybe—
"crazy eyes"—
a look I can assume
that actors use for mad scenes
in "meaty" parts.
Jumping when ground's too hot to stand on,
when the sound goes off,
when words don't come
to signal train is stopping,
skin has turned to wood.

Moving mouths.
Hands picking at emptiness.
His soul hiding in the corner,
run out of space—
still seeing when you look away.

Eat, inhale, exhale madness.
A tradition choking off poets
whose brains become dice.
Do the mad receive justice
with sword stampeding mind?

There is the door
where brains become dice,
where we have chemicals
to take you back and forth.
Can you put on shoes,
buy at stores with blanked imagination?
See peace in sun-filled street?

This street two blocks from home—
small park, dark candy store—
that children cross,
is his outer edge of health,
her safer side of dreams.

In the Mail

He wrote the letter to his father,
forty pages Kafka wrote.
My father said, "I'll write a letter,
I'll write you a letter,""
to all questions over and under.
He never did,
and saying's done.

Letters lie like plates on table,
like late excuses
not arriving, reviving sight wounds.
Ink-fisted letters talk,
pass pain through stamps in mail.

His father didn't receive it.
Kafka saved it to indict himself
as lawyer-liar.
"Which I am," he wrote,
wanting word axes
to break silent self in heartless half.
My father/Kafka,
I, still believing—
opening books,
not hearing hardened words—
send love.

Art Process

For Eva Hesse: 1936-1970

Scatterings on floor, rubber cuts,
shattering glass,
break-through time perhaps, or maybe not.

We have shadows, pieces, films
of acts called art
that were about life, or maybe not.

See Eva's feeling for
ropes and teguments,
for frames of pain that took her
beyond what she could know.
Flowering tumors, translucent curtains,
last art covering:
mix and pour
outside forms of inside boundaries
made of bodies that were, or maybe not.

"Hand tossing lead,"
catching and missing.
Lead time filmed in minutes tossing:
this act, his life,
what sculptors do, or maybe not.

But she didn't roll lead, make finger marks—
what the hand could do
that life wouldn't.
Wanting to start again,
be Eva always, or maybe not.

Leanings: after Eva, another sculptor
and meetings of tongue and groove,
art and love.
He waves and goes
and Eva, gathering up her grievings,
builds joinings of fanatic pain
to strew across a floor.

Manet's Boats

For Joan Marter

They didn't sail,
moving over green grass purple,
stuck on lumpy waves,
not seen.
One more subject:
dead matador across a canvas weighs,
his costume a painting,
while bodies are themselves.
Meanwhile, the sea contains
and Manet sees
at the station, near the gate,
the woman in white mirror dress all
   shining steam.
Sad face, soft body
turning inward,
the flesh, not trees, are home.
His eyes, the creeping black
   of bedroom night,
the room, his moment—
a window to filter in the day
on couch settee,
from where he watched her watching,
move of painted ocean,
Manet's eye, Morisot's eye
and Olympia's still afloat.

Verbal Question

It isn't content
but way of registering
how many rust purple columns keep out third rail,
of noting
three-minute air-warnings of coming train.
Under the depression hat under your hair,
blank starts in an on-going process
signal out sharp black/white cord string,
blue/white shirt,
striped surroundings I wear.
Subway riders tell themselves stories
in striped shirts, skirts, pants not seeing—
on tracks between lines above the third rail
with us not seeing.

Content,
objects of feeling.
When feeling halts,
eyes close windows while I cross streets,
Break-up crashes all inside,
colors blur glass of slide,
head moves so slowly
pills speed down pain while things
accept an afternoon's death,
Holding out a word.

Meaning is content:
objects pile up:
edges of tan car seat, of man's hairy elbow,
gold watch on girl's black arm—
arm which is brown purple—
closed eyes in silent shut-down.
Of sleep, no content—
no content during gear change for
junk heaps, auto graves,
city dumps full of content
still chasing meaning.

Intoxication

Intoxication isn't art,
closes off paintings,
sounds at parties.
A before-spring place,
lips opening.
Arrives in leather.
waves M.T. V. moments,
where catch breath,
rescue falling, and
float love.

Finger-ends touch world—
and my pen writes tongues
in floats of clear moment.
Single horn sounds
'Be drunken'
soars, dives,
meets in non-arrival.

In toxic smile unto,
always being urgent—
"Welcome to Joust,
Beware of the unbearable pterodactyl.
The highest lance wins in a collision.
Meet thy enemies.
We are not interested in temporary safety,"—
but in games of joy.

Country

Entity, country, breath—
whose beginning?
Who's belonging?
Yellow shoes, purple tight clear color choice,
flag of my heart.
They want lives only sometime,
acreage their definition.
Go seek land on mirror's other side,
yet country remains.
I, yes, we, the keepers singing.

Unmapped Geographies

Mirror lakes, old castles, newer camps,
land where my cousins died.
Language of branching words,
mind power,
secret meanings interconnect to grail,
salute. I run.
Mad monster haunts Germany,
hunting me.

Blond princesses, porcelain-boned and thin-
mouthed
with full-cheeked children
are beautiful. Why be afraid?
These words are children's forests of unreason,
grounds for poetry,
on shifting wind.
Incense burned to innocence and death.

Siegfried's horn smokes on,
somewhere in Brecht's Mahagonny town,
where mad, sick, Nietzsche laughs—
these are friends.
I see into Mann's magic past,
remembering Hebrew Joseph,
and far off, think music in scrubbed kitchen.

Floor sheen, horn song.
Organized personages don't breathe—
This being a favorite lie.
But German—German is a word,
a place of cities, cliche of order, fact-
  efficient,
non-wasting time,
skin stretched to no waste—

Not now. Before.
—And not their memory.

Bridge Disconnectors, No. I 1983
24″ H × 36″ L Oil on Paper

VKW I "Bridge Connectors" HELMAN '87

Bridge Disconnectors, No. II 1983
24″ H × 36″ L Oil on Paper

HELMAN

Bridge Disconnectors, No. III 1983
24″ H × 36″ L Oil on Paper

IEW III "Bridges. Connectors"
HELMAN

Bridge Disconnectors, No. IV 1983
24″ H × 36″ L Oil on Paper

HELMAN

Bridge Disconnectors, No. V 1983
24″ H × 36″ L Oil on Paper

HELMAN

Bridge Disconnectors, No. VII 1983
24″ H × 36″ L Oil on Paper

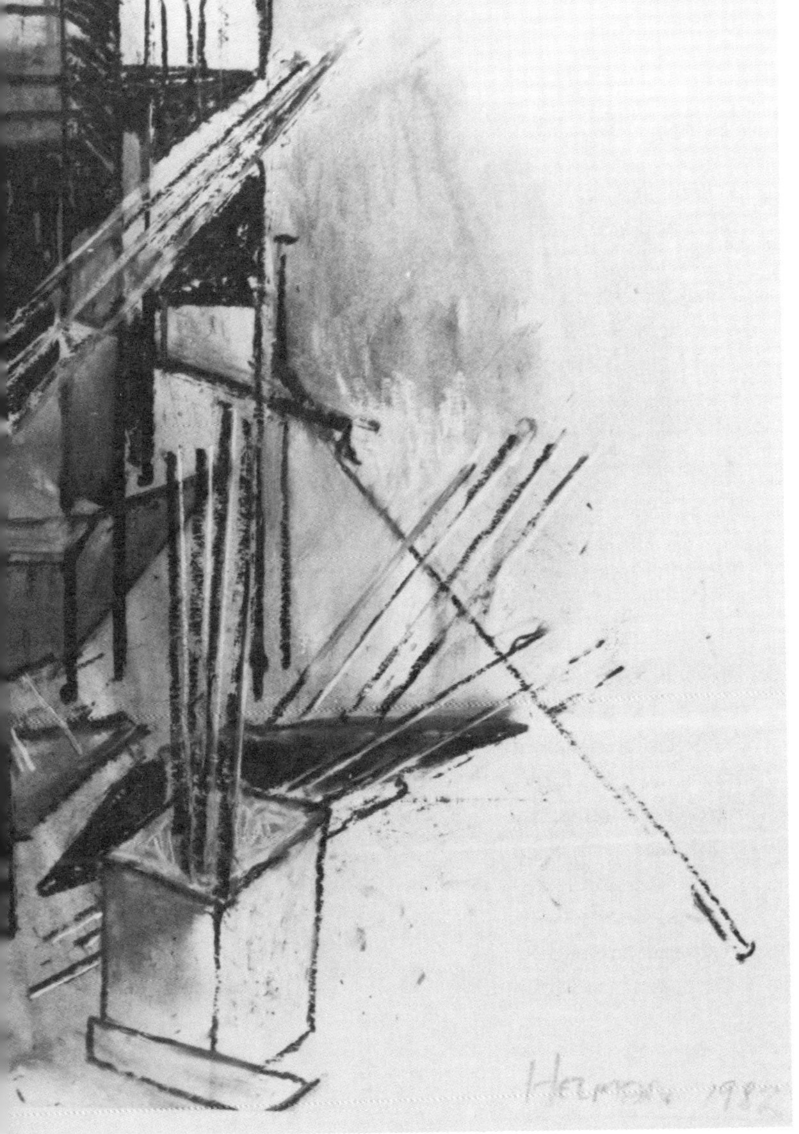

In the Nest

Where we were—
older and younger,
bigger, smaller—
I walking behind
coming from thick-walled rooms,
A girl in front with thin, straight legs.
I can see my sister anywhere:
two girls stand on the sidewalk;
myself, the smaller,
stubby-legged and smiling
at beautiful sky, pavement squares,
hopscotch map.

Outside, she is Leader.
Tall buildings guard us,
trees tied to plots.
Public children standing
in new-washed clothes,
together run on leads.
In the dark,
animal skin and hair,
voice calls across beds,
finger-ends are real—
where she goes, I follow.

Bright sunlight,
similar eyes, identical hand moves.
Two sisters lunch outside,
their unshared lives
hide each other's memories
of dark times, nightmare spaces,
sharp edges of being young.
And the older,
because always there,
still through their lives
moves first.

Adolescence

The girls with dark eyes and new skins
run in the water, gathering.
They are—things of their world.
What is woman's space?
Born with a skin,
with other eyes looking,
sudden deer dancers
locked to the moon,
to an egg under sun's certainty.
Coloring of skins,
day and night rhythms,
girls—
delight of a big-bellied lady
reaching through unsettled dust
to a run on the road,
a moment sky-touched, the stars—
before the slow promenade
of mother life starts.

The Affair Song

Trust the day,
not rising blood, but presence of sky.
Nothing lasts like rock,
like the edges of inconvenient boulders
somewhere up on Mars.

The lie from your mouth,
a tooth cutting my tongue.
Ordinary as a daily murder. Nothing lasts.
See, only numbers make the news.

A rock lives in a cardboard house.
You make a bed of promises,
sing sweet songs
and put me down to sleep.

I wake on broken glass
to hear truths everyone knows.
Wanting to dance your lies,
my eyes, hurt stones,
hoping nothing lasts.

Letter Not To Be Sent Abroad

For Joyce

At 18, you are not immune,
have only age and us on your side.
The *Young Hegelians* play tonight at CBGB's,
one more philosopher rock-band combo
who you, not us, would know.

Across the water, over the air
I look for your new world,
watching from the sidewalk.

You've gone six hours and thirty years ahead,
while I've been learning what time is
by the changed feel of your skin.

Here, singing radios surround me,
ice cream men and mechanical birds follow the beat.
Children run, salt taste, hard grit
under the sun lock me to this moment.
Here, six hours and two languages away
I write you in English from Spanish New York,
knowing even if all the transitors die
and planes overhead fly away,
the other languages,
the time/space roads you travel,
will keep us out of hearing.

Even so, we wait—
a phone call is your untouching hand
soothing us,
something to have as our two wave,
"Restez tranquille, be well, take care,"
from the other side of life.

Between Waves

Can I make poetry from this imbecile heat
after fireworks cease flowering in our faces
while their smoky webs stay in my mind?
Missing the black sky
because too many street lamps are in the way,
stepping out on ambulance paths,
a bare-backed woman climbing the wall
Independence Day night, running from July summer.

Imbecile heat and fan sounds clog late evening hours.
Walking by grid-locked cars
through streets of nervous policemen
at work on the Glorious 4th,
while Little Italy rockets in smoke
and Soho in punkster couples:
a matched pair with shaved heads, hard nails
and circle eyes, sporting rhinestone ties.

We're doing the 4th.
Eyes burn in unmoving air.
Applauding the lights,
applauding ourselves standing here
in year of Europe get-aways.
Women with children in strollers push forward,
men carrying babies move on. Couples swaying,
partying on the 4th, on the street
among nervous policemen.

The heat follows. Doing the 4th—
convalescents from heat-reamed sky,
beach victims after weekends of stopped breath
roll us to jungle,
where animals know to sleep thirsting under the day
and run in shining dark.
But now, after flowering lights,
snake smoke and roars east and west,
another thunder is promised, and
rain, coming with shifting winds.

The End of My Dog

Lost is gone,
except in mind corners
and where the body remembers—
the missing habit
under the desk,
near the couch—a presence
whose sleep is gone.

Levels in the room
lived by other tribes,
four-footed dwellers
passing and re-passing.
Language of car sound.
Your sound being car word,
sound meaning food, garbage can,
  footstep
of stairway enemy now gone.

You dream running.
Four legs go and
tail, one more move sounding
till the break.
First day of autumn;
I listen to radiator hiss
and winter start
in new silence.

Birthday Poem

Hard prints under the eyes,
body strings loosening.
The age of half a life.
Rhythms, habits, measuring what's left
isn't a magic song for new beginnings.
Meaning—
I can't be beautiful or young,
love anyone again in bits and pieces
over twenty years.
Meaning—
I can flare up,
enough still here,
life's last third,
a new beginning,
which is good, because
the day's strangeness seems still ahead;
that light, that flying flag
just coming into reach.

Invisible Books

Mine live in boxes
telling art-world stories,
muttering about love.

Are tied up carrying
someone's belongings,
the body of a body,
memories lost in intent,
day of, time of.

Ghost hopes went along,
draping those stories
with medals for, pleasures at—
words out of heart dust.

Under the coat, an inside pocket.
Run down the stairs,
invisible books blowing round my ears.
A woman split in two,
looking in the mirror.

Inside paper stack,
a glory-chasing gray man
cries for his past, for its misses.
I fill white sheets
with his forgotten lies.

Would you like, do I—
unbound time papers:
books of no measure,
talking madness, art, desire,
youngness of all wanting,
live mute in their box embrace.

Prescription

1.

Swallowed pills, jumping presences,
alien nerves invade sight,
head pressing in
as they breathe beside me,
pushing panic,
whose rhythms keep rest off.

A beating here in place.
No going forward, but a fear—
their will, the chemical stuff
breaking, its presence dissolving,
until this cityscape of even, upright houses,
of rusting columns and ordered window panes
falls back before rising food smell,
mixes brain fumes, pills and beating mind
by way of scientific cure.

2.

I establish the territory
ordered by heart breathing into future.
Beginning early morning
this series of swallowed storms will pass—
War orders:
I drink the waters,
body weather fighting chemistry.

These Were Palaces 1984
84″ L × 72″ H collage paint

Mister Charm Returns

We meet again,
looking for past selves.
I, middle-aged,
you, street man, super con,
hating half the world
for being hole and opening,
but forgiving an old friend.

You boast you're brother rat,
lighting on weakness,
tearing at young,
eating dreams before they can be made,
between grimaces
you pour out before me
word torrents evoking love.

I press my lips,
nodding at street litanies,
salvation words that toe-dance
to all systems.
I, a mother, listening
as you con man, con lover,
seeking innocence,
evoke your days with boy children,
your games of playing trickster Christ
to their hope of God.

The angel of death is beautiful.
Stones in the park still quiet,
where we had suicide talks
thirty years ago, seeking a direction.
You, beginning drunk,
playing on disturbance,
opting for what I didn't know.

I gave up that angel
who today you claim,
with distended belly and nervous walk,
announcing you've an heir:
"Am adopting a boy your daughter's age,
my lover—
a little mad, who lives much in his own mind,"
you say, exhibiting concern.
Will it suffice then, for you to be his mother?

Child molesters reign supreme
in certain streets, addresses known,
seeking delicate skins to cut,
unshaped minds to close,
seeking to be within themselves an end,
while I can't think who to call.

Lies must sever, laws be bent.
Prison man talking writing
across the table
touts a literature revoking God
for making women mothers.

But I knew yours
and you at fifteen
come from dunghills full of money,
fleas of the Yiddish proverb
swarming around you.
"Not decent, honest people,"
My father said.

While you made me laugh,
turning us to stilt-walkers
yelling across exchanges
so as to love, not touch,
working up each other's fever,
safe in public streets.

Exultation isn't real.
Even while you gave certainty
we were immortal.
We didn't know
fleas of Yiddish proverb
would attend your charm.
Couldn't know age would become
   drunken sex,
a life-long scam which today
you re-invent
in descriptions of your victims.

I listen
because moral judgments are only walls,
and the warmth of a parasite presence,
of even a converse love,
is also life.

Numero Uno

"Numero uno," faces:
my face in mirrors changing,
cat paws admiring twin,
looks away.
what comes back limits self-stance.
Images run together:
Faces in movie bathrooms,
in gray lights inside darkness;
tired strangers talking,
heavy-set girl watching people,
stringy woman's eyes crease with aging look,
with fear of own strangeness—
That's who's come so far.

Waking still a girl,
film over window,
light not quite so bright,
ozone layers cut off sharpness,
magic detail gets away.
At forty, turning mean,
ten o'clock sun paints up building,
and behind light,
in warmth, hides.

Known faces,
beyond prettiness of children's cheeks,
eyes celebrating animal questions.
My own, with feature definition,
geographic character, geologic lines
in soft skin grain
is thinned.
Moderate triumph through time.

Friends, enemies
marvel at each other's looks,
our tribe having learned
to accept mirrors clocking lives,
to celebrate seeming rock-like
before becoming nothing.

Incantation

Trees are upright silences,
safety signs,
their leaves broken promises
to still the brain
amid cars, trucks and sidewalks,
the human, bleeding world,
the trap of days
before the quiet earth will come.

Motor runs, heel taps.
I hear me, my enemy,
hunting down my life.
Pronoun play: we three
who make a self don't break,
don't help, don't save,
beneath three trees are safe
amid their quiet breathing,
moving presences not strange.
This lie to travel with
through hounded afternoons.

CORINNE ROBINS, poet, critic and author of THE PLURALIST ERA: *American Art 1968-1981* (Harper & Row, 1984), and FIRST, a book of poems (Pratt Press, 1983). She is a Visiting Associate Professor at Pratt Institute.

PHOEBE HELMAN has had numerous one-person shows in New York City and throughout the country. Winner of a National Endowment Award, a Guggenheim Award and two CAPS Fellowships, she is a permanent member of the Art Faculty of Pratt Institute.